A Guide to
AMERICAN STATES

Washington

THE EVERGREEN STATE

AV² provides enriched content that supplements and complements this book. Weigl's AV² books strive to create inspired learning and engage young minds in a total learning experience.

Your AV² Media Enhanced books come alive with...

Audio
Listen to sections of the book read aloud.

Key Words
Study vocabulary, and complete a matching word activity.

Video
Watch informative video clips.

Quizzes
Test your knowledge.

Embedded Weblinks
Gain additional information for research.

Slide Show
View images and captions, and prepare a presentation.

Go to **www.av2books.com**, and enter this book's unique code.

BOOK CODE

Y 4 9 7 7 4 3

AV² by Weigl brings you media enhanced books that support active learning.

Try This!
Complete activities and hands-on experiments.

... and much, much more!

Published by AV² by Weigl
350 5th Avenue, 59th Floor
New York, NY 10118
Website: www.av2books.com   www.weigl.com

Library of Congress Cataloging-in-Publication Data

Strudwick, Leslie, 1970-
 Washington / Leslie Strudwick.
   p. cm. -- (A guide to American states)
 Includes index.
 ISBN 978-1-61690-820-1 (hardcover : alk. paper) -- ISBN 978-1-61690-496-8 (online)
 1. Washington (State)--Juvenile literature. I. Title.
 F891.3.S773 2011
 979.7--dc23
                                    2011019237

Printed in the United States of America in North Mankato, Minnesota

052011
WEP180511

Project Coordinator Jordan McGill
Art Director Terry Paulhus

Photo Credits
Every reasonable effort has been made to trace ownership and to obtain permission to reprint copyright material. The publishers would be pleased to have any errors or omissions brought to their attention so that they may be corrected in subsequent printings.

Weigl acknowledges Getty Images as its primary image supplier for this title.
Photo of Abraham Lincoln Presidential Library and Museum on page 20 courtesy of Edward A. Thomas.

Contents

The Space Needle gives Seattle one of the best-known skylines in the world.

Introduction

A lthough it is known as the Evergreen State, Washington has far more to offer than its trees. There are many lakes, towering mountains, and diverse natural regions. Along with Oregon and part of Idaho, Washington lies in the Pacific Northwest region of the United States. This area has rugged landscapes, abundant wildlife, and a rich American Indian heritage.

The history of Washington is closely tied to that of Oregon, its neighbor to the south. Many of the region's first settlers of European heritage traveled to the Pacific Northwest along the Oregon Trail. This pioneer trail ran from Independence, Missouri, to the Columbia River region along the border between present-day Washington and Oregon.

Colorful wildflowers are found throughout the state.

The state is home to many types of wildlife, including mule deer. The deer gets its name from its long, mule-like ears.

First used by fur traders and missionaries, the trail was suddenly, in the 1840s, thick with the wagon trains of thousands of settlers. At first the newcomers mainly stopped in the Willamette River Valley of what became the state of Oregon. Gradually they moved into the area north of the Columbia River, in what is now Washington.

In 1848 the U.S. Congress established the Oregon Territory, which included all of the present-day states of Oregon, Washington, and Idaho and parts of Wyoming and Montana. As the population around Puget Sound grew, settlers urged the government to form a separate territory north and west of the Columbia. In 1853, Congress created the Washington Territory, including parts of present-day Idaho and Montana. The territory was named in honor of George Washington, the first president of the United States. The creation of the Idaho Territory in 1863 reduced Washington to its present boundaries. Finally, in 1889, Washington was admitted to the Union as the 42nd state.

Where Is Washington?

Washington is located in the northwestern corner of the **contiguous** 48 U.S. states. Visitors can reach the state by many forms of transportation. Many major airlines fly into both of the state's main airports, Seattle-Tacoma International and Spokane International. A network of highways and other roads takes people to all corners of the state and beyond. By train, visitors can enter Washington from the north, south, or east. Ferries connect places along Washington's west coast with one another and with destinations in Canada.

Washington's most important river, the Columbia River, provides a route for large, oceangoing vessels. Flowing south from Canada, the Columbia enters the northeastern part of Washington and winds throughout the state. The river is an important source of **hydroelectric power**.

The Mount St. Helens volcano, which erupted in 1980, is located in Skamania County. It is part of the Cascade Range.

Washington is well recognized for its beautiful scenery and wildlife. However, the people of the state also contribute to its popularity. Microsoft founder Bill Gates, who ranks as one of the richest people in the world, helped put the Seattle area on the map as a center for high technology. In the 1990s Seattle was also a trendsetter in the music industry. Many **grunge** bands were formed, following the lead of Seattle bands such as Nirvana and Pearl Jam.

Another famous name in Washington is Mount St. Helens. In May 1980 this volcano erupted for the first time in 123 years. The eruption sent ash 12 miles into the air. Many towns were blanketed by volcanic ash. Airborne ash covered 22,000 square miles, and some of the ash drifted as far east as Montana. This disaster was one of the most violent volcanic eruptions ever recorded in North America.

The scenic Columbia River Gorge forms part of the border between Washington to the north and Oregon to the south. The gorge is 80 miles long and up to 4,000 feet deep.

Mapping Washington

Washington is bordered by Oregon to the south and Idaho to the east. The Pacific Ocean lies to the west, and the Canadian province of British Columbia is to the north. The Cascade Range, a chain of mountains in western Washington, adds majesty to the state's landscape. Puget Sound, a large inlet, is located in Washington's northwestern corner.

Sites and Symbols

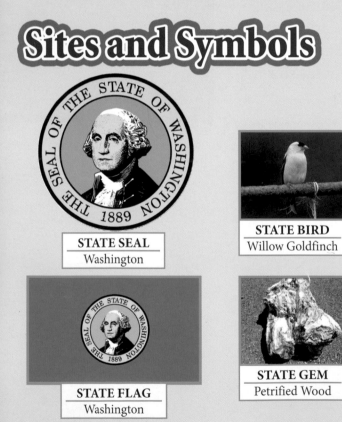

STATE SEAL
Washington

STATE BIRD
Willow Goldfinch

STATE FLOWER
Coast
Rhododendron

STATE FLAG
Washington

STATE GEM
Petrified Wood

STATE TREE
Western Hemlock

Nickname The Evergreen State

Motto *Alki* (By and By)

Song "Washington, My Home," written by Helen Davis and arranged by Stuart Churchill

Entered the Union November 11, 1889, as the 42nd state

Capital Olympia

Population (2010 Census) 6,724,540 Ranked 13th state

BRITISH COLUMBIA

Blaine
Ferndale
Bellingham
Mount Vernon
Port Townsend
North Marysville
Forks
Port Angeles
Everett
Seattle
Bellevue
Renton
Kent
Shelton
Tacoma
Lakes District
Aberdeen
Olympia
Raymond
Centralia
Castle Rock
Kelso
Warrenton
Seaside
Woodland
Scappoose
Vancouver
Portland
Tigard
Gresham
Woodburn

Pacific Ocean

Oroville
Tonasket
Marcus
Colville
Okanogan
Brewster
Chewelah
Newport
Sandpoint
Chelan
Deer Park
Athol
Entiat
Creston
Almira
Spokane
Wenatchee
WASHINGTON
Opportunity
Roslyn
Rosalia
Ellensburg
George
Moses Lake
Ritzville
Colfax
Pullman
Moscow
Connell
Yakima
Toppenish
Richland
Pasco
Clarkston
Lewiston
Grandview
Prosser
Dayton
Walla Walla
Goldendale
Hood River
Hermiston
Pendleton
The Dalles
Rufus
Arlington
Pilot Rock
Grass Valley

IDAHO

OREGON

LEGEND

— Road
— River
⭐ State Capital
● City
▢ Washington
— State Border

Map Scale

0   100 Miles

N

STATE CAPITAL

The capital of Washington is Olympia, at the southern end of Puget Sound. It became the capital of the Washington Territory in 1853 and was kept as the state capital when Washington entered the Union in 1889.

United States

Washington

Hawai'i   Alaska

The Land

The greatest feature of Washington's landscape is the Cascade Range. This mountain chain runs from north to south and divides the state into two parts. About one-third of the state lies west of the Cascades. The area around Puget Sound is a lowland that contains more than half of the state's population. In the northwest are the Olympic Mountains, and in the southwest are the Willapa Hills. The largest region east of the Cascades is the Columbia Plateau. The Okanogan Highlands in the northeast are an extension of the Rocky Mountains. The Blue Mountains cover the southeastern corner of the state.

PUGET SOUND

Puget Sound is a deep inlet of the Pacific Ocean that stretches 100 miles. Its maximum depth is 930 feet.

MOUNT OLYMPUS

The highest peak in the Olympic Mountains is Mount Olympus. It is 7,962 feet high.

SAN JUAN ISLANDS

The San Juan Islands are an **archipelago** of more than 170 islands scattered around upper Puget Sound. Visitors come to the islands to enjoy outdoor activities such as hiking, sailing, and scuba diving.

COLUMBIA RIVER

East of the Cascades, the Columbia River runs through the dry Columbia Plateau. The Columbia is the largest river in the Pacific Northwest.

I DIDN'T KNOW THAT!

The Ice Harbor Dam, which was completed in 1961, is located on the Snake River. Lake Sacajawea is formed behind the dam.

One of the cloudiest towns in the United States is in Washington. Quillayute is cloudy an average of 239 days a year.

The place where the Columbia River empties into the Pacific Ocean is called Cape Disappointment. It is home to Cape Disappointment State Park.

The highest temperature ever recorded in Washington occurred on August 5, 1961, at Ice Harbor Dam. It was 118° Fahrenheit.

The air blowing in from the Pacific Ocean keeps summer temperatures down along Washington's western coast. The state's coastal residents enjoy breezy, mild summers.

Climate

The Cascade Range creates two very different climate areas in Washington. West of the Cascades winters are mild and summers are warm. Rain falls throughout the year, with snow falling mainly near the mountains. On the eastern side of the Cascades, summers are hot and dry, but winters are cold and snow is common.

Average rainfall is just 6 to 10 inches per year in the eastern part of the state, but it is more than 60 inches per year near the west coast. Some parts of the state receive more than 100 inches of precipitation every year.

Average Annual Precipitation Across Washington

The amount of precipitation in a typical year tends to vary greatly from place to place in Washington, depending on where in the state a city or town is located. Why might Quillayute receive much more rainfall than Seattle?

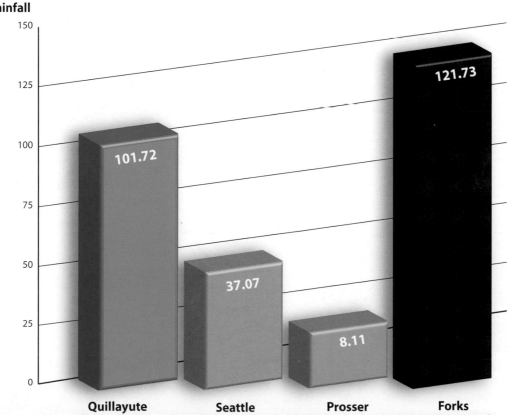

Inches of Rainfall

	Quillayute	Seattle	Prosser	Forks
	101.72	37.07	8.11	121.73

Natural Resources

Washington is rich in natural resources. The most important resources are lumber, water, and fish. There is much debate in the state over the use of these resources. Over the years industries and people have caused pollution, cut down forests, fished the waters, and drained rivers to irrigate fields. Industries began to **deplete** the state's natural resources. Measures have been taken to protect the environment. Many industries continue to use the state's natural resources, but **environmentalists** have worked hard to control the level of harm to the environment. Washington still has beautiful forests, rich soil, many rivers and lakes, and abundant wildlife.

Washington is known for its beautiful scenery. It is often listed as the "greenest" state in the country.

Washington's ground also holds important mineral resources. Zinc and lead are mined in small amounts in the state. The country's largest reserve of **olivine** is mined near the Twin Sisters mountains. The most **plentiful** of the state's mined products are sand and gravel. Both are used in construction. Gemstones mined in Washington include opals, agate, and amethyst.

Commercial fishing brings millions of dollars to the state every year.

I DIDN'T KNOW THAT!

In the past some of Washington's forests have been clear-cut by the timber industry, leaving bare patches of land.

Washington's long coastline makes fishing a valuable part of the state's economy.

There are three national parks, three national historical parks, and three national recreation areas in Washington.

Irrigation is a common practice for farmers in eastern Washington who need more water than is naturally available.

Plants

Trees cover much of the western part of Washington. Western hemlock and Douglas fir are most plentiful, especially at the lower elevations. Other tree species include mountain hemlock and Pacific silver fir.

It is impossible to observe Washington's plant life without considering the state's ancient rain forest. Washington's Olympic Peninsula has some of the world's largest trees, including Sitka spruce, western red cedar, Douglas fir, and western hemlock. Most of them are about 200 feet high, but some trees grow as tall as 300 feet. The ground and most of the trees are covered in moss, which thrives in areas of high rainfall.

Eastern Washington has far fewer trees. In the more northern mountains, there are ponderosa pines. The southern farmland area is dominated by prairie **vegetation** such as sagebrush and grasses.

COAST RHODODENDRON

Washington's state flower, the coast rhododendron, is also called the western or pink rhododendron. The word *rhododendron* means "rose tree."

LUPINE

The lupine, a member of the pea family, can be found throughout Washington. The lupine's flowers can be pink, blue, white, or a mixture of these colors.

WESTERN HEMLOCK

The state tree of Washington, the western hemlock, is a type of pine tree. Its reddish-brown bark was used by American Indians for dyeing objects and tanning leather.

HUCKLEBERRY BUSHES

Twelve species of huckleberry can be found in the Pacific Northwest. Products made with huckleberries, such as jams and candies, are sold throughout Washington.

More than 3,000 kinds of wildflowers grow in the state of Washington.

The western hemlock is also known as the Pacific hemlock, the hemlock spruce, the Prince Albert's fir, or the Alaskan pine.

The trees in the Olympic rain forest have never been logged.

Animals

Wild animals can be found in all parts of Washington. The state's varied habitats support many types of animals, including mountain lions, mountain goats, mule deer, elk, and coyotes. Washington is known as a bird-watcher's paradise. One of the most notable and common sights is a bald eagle. Thousands of these eagles spend the winter just north of Seattle on the Skagit River. They share the sky with hundreds of other bird species, including owls, hawks, and smaller birds such as robins and finches.

The water is also rich in wildlife. Salmon live in the state's many rivers. Crabs, lobsters, oysters, and clams share the coastal waters with killer whales and gray whales. Whale-watching boat trips are available for people interested in seeing these huge mammals swim, feed, and play in the ocean.

HARBOR SEAL

Harbor seals can grow to be 7 feet long and can weigh more than 200 pounds. Many harbor seals make their home in Puget Sound.

KILLER WHALE

Killer whales, or orcas, are a popular attraction along the Washington coast. They are related to dolphins and travel in groups called pods. Many visitors enjoy whale watching trips.

BALD EAGLE

Bald eagles feed on the fish in Washington's rivers and streams. These birds were once **endangered**, but their numbers made a comeback thanks to help from environmental groups.

MOUNTAIN LION

The mountain lion is the largest cat found in the state. About 2,500 live in the wild, but these solitary animals are rarely seen.

I DIDN'T KNOW THAT!

Black bears can be seen in Olympic National Park.

Washington is home to many endangered animals, including the woodland caribou, the grizzly bear, the gray wolf, and the Columbian white-tailed deer.

Oystercatchers use their long, red-orange bills to pry open the shells of oysters.

Tourism

Tourism is a growing industry in Washington. With so many state and national parks, Washington has an array of natural areas where people can hike, camp, ski, bike, fish, and boat. Hiking is popular with visitors and residents alike. Hikers on Washington's superb trails can follow streams and rivers, cross valleys, climb mountains, or discover towering redwood forests.

One popular tourist spot is Mount St. Helens, where visitors can learn about volcanoes. Tourists can hire a helicopter or plane to fly over the Mount St. Helens and look down into the crater. Mount Rainier is another active volcano, but it is covered by ice. Mount Baker is a popular ski area.

Seattle, Washington's largest city, attracts many visitors to its museums, restaurants, festivals, and sporting events. Famous for its fresh fish, farm produce, and shops, the Pike Place Market covers nine acres on Seattle's waterfront. Boat tours depart daily from nearby piers.

OLYMPIC NATIONAL PARK

A large part of the Olympic Mountains can be viewed in Olympic National Park. Visitors come from all over the world to hike the park's many trails.

SPACE NEEDLE

The Space Needle is one of Seattle's most famous landmarks. Built for the 1962 World's Fair, it stands 605 feet high. Visitors can go to the top for spectacular views of the city and surrounding area.

SEATTLE AQUARIUM

More than 20 million people have come to the Seattle Aquarium since it opened in 1977. The aquarium has an underwater dome that holds 400,000 gallons of water.

PIKE PLACE MARKET

Pike Place Market has been in operation for more than 100 years. Approximately 10 million people visit the market every year.

The natural arch at Rialto Beach is a popular attraction in Olympic National Park.

The Space Needle has a revolving restaurant, Sky City, which completes a full turn every hour.

Scenic Point Defiance Park in Tacoma is one of the largest city parks in the United States. About 2 million people visit the park every year.

The first monorail in the United States was built in Seattle, for the 1962 World's Fair. As part of the city's mass-transit system, it carries about 2.5 million people each year.

Industry

The **aerospace industry** is one of the largest in the state. The Boeing Company was founded by William Boeing in the Seattle area in 1916. In the first half of the 20th century, Boeing built planes for the U.S. armed forces in both World War I and World War II. The company then turned its focus toward **commercial** jets, satellites, missile systems, and newer, more advanced military aircraft. Boeing's final-assembly plant is located in Everett.

Industries in Washington
Value of Goods and Services in Millions of Dollars

The media and entertainment industry in Washington accounts for almost one-tenth of the economy, a higher proportion than in most other states. This industry includes software publishing. Why is it such a large industry in Washington?

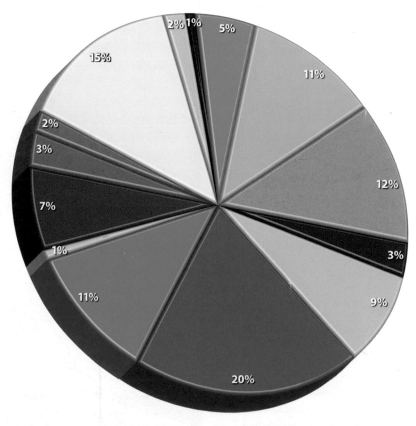

LEGEND

	Agriculture, Forestry, and Fishing	$6,061
*	Mining	$722
	Utilities	$3,979
	Construction	$15,333
	Manufacturing	$38,058
	Wholesale and Retail Trade	$41,089
	Transportation	$8,851
	Media and Entertainment	$30,628
	Finance, Insurance, and Real Estate	$66,059
	Professional and Technical Services	$35,862
	Education	$1,892
	Health Care	$22,110
	Hotels and Restaurants	$8,990
	Other Services	$8,117
	Government	$50,583
	TOTAL	**$338,334**

*Less than 1%. Percentages may not add to 100 because of rounding.

Another sector of the economy that has grown over the years is the software industry. Microsoft was founded in Seattle in the 1970s and became the leading software producing company in the nation. The company has its headquarters in Redmond. More than 40,000 employees work at this location. Washington's other major industries include shipping, food processing, logging, fishing, and agriculture.

Microsoft's headquarters in Redmond is called the Microsoft Corporate Campus. The campus contains a baseball diamond, a basketball court, and a large collection of fine art.

Microsoft Corporation is one of the most successful companies in the United States. The name Microsoft is a combination of the words microcomputer and software.

The Boeing plant in Everett is one of the largest enclosed spaces in the world. It needs to be large enough to house wide-body jumbo passenger jets for assembly.

Many of the products and much of the food processed in Washington are sent to Asian countries such as Japan, China, Singapore, and South Korea.

Washington's tourism industry earned almost $16 billion in 2008.

Some high schools in Seattle offer an Academy of Hospitality and Tourism program. Students who take part in this program can learn about careers in the tourism industry.

Goods and Services

Washington's fertile soil is responsible for its strong agricultural output. The state produces a wide range of fruits and vegetables. Washington's fresh produce is distributed across the state and all over the world. Three of Washington's biggest crops are apples, potatoes, and wheat. Washington grows more apples than any other state. In 2009, about 19 million pounds of apples were produced in the United States. More than half of those apples came from Washington. The state's specialty is Red Delicious apples.

Other crops grown in Washington include cherries, raspberries, pears, asparagus, spearmint, and peppermint. Most of the peppermint crop is used to make peppermint oil. The state's farmers also raise livestock, which is sold for food. The most common types of livestock raised in the state are chickens, turkeys, cattle, hogs, and sheep.

Starbucks Coffee opened its first store in Pike Place Market in 1971. The store is still operating today.

Although Washington farmers grow a great deal of food, fewer than 3 percent of the state's workers are employed in agriculture. About 11 percent work in manufacturing. But far more of the state's residents work in the service sector of the economy. Workers in this sector provide some form of assistance or service to other people. Many people in this sector work as computer programmers or in restaurants. Others are employed in wholesale or retail businesses.

Washington's Red Delicious apples are harvested in September and October, but they are stored so they can be available to shoppers year-round.

Washington is one of the top states in exports to countries in Africa, Asia, and the European Union.

Seafood lovers come from around the world to sample Washington's fresh fish.

The town of Zillah has the oldest operating gas station in the country, which was built in 1922. It is shaped like a teapot.

American Indians

Before the arrival of people of European descent, many different American Indian groups lived in what is now Washington. Their living conditions and what they ate were influenced by where they lived. The coastal groups included the Makah, the Quinault, the Skokomish, the Skagit, the Lummi, and the Snohomish. They were skilled fishers and hunters of seals and whales. They obtained much of their food from the sea. Their homes and boats were built from huge cedar trees that grew in the area.

The Nez Percé lived east of the Cascades. They moved their homes depending on the seasons, going to places where they could find food easily.

East of the Cascade Range were the Okanagan, the Colville, the Spokane, the Yakama, the Nez Percé, and the Palouse. These groups had to travel farther in their search for food. They hunted rabbit, deer, and elk, and they caught salmon. They lived in large pits that they dug in the ground and covered with roofs of grass or branches. These deep pit houses protected them from the wind and the cold.

The Chinook were a link between the eastern and the western Indian groups, as well as traders traveling between California and what is now the Yukon Territory of Canada. They lived along the Columbia River and were mostly traders. Their exchanges with many types of people led to Chinook Jargon, a language that could be understood by many different peoples in the region.

American Indians made their homes in Washington for thousands of years before explorers began to arrive.

The Yakama were hunter-gathers. They were forced onto a **reservation** in 1858.

Today there are more than 20 American Indian reservations across the state.

The Makah attached sealskin balloons to their whale harpoons to prevent pierced whales from diving and swimming away.

Many Nez Percé lived in structures that could house several families. These dwellings are called longhouses.

Explorers and Missionaries

The first explorers in the region from the United States were fur traders. One of them was Robert Gray, captain of the *Columbia Rediviva*. In 1792, Gray sailed into the mouth of a great river, which he named the Columbia River, after his ship. Following Gray's voyage, the United States claimed the region. President Thomas Jefferson knew about the region's profitable fur trade. In the early 1800s he sent an expedition led by Meriwether Lewis and William Clark to explore and map a route from the Mississippi River to the Pacific Ocean. This new route allowed traders and settlers to travel to the Far West by land as well as by sea.

Along with fur traders came missionaries. These people wanted to teach Christianity to the American Indians in the area. Two early missionaries were Marcus and Narcissa Whitman. They lived in peace with the Cayuse until 1847, when an epidemic of measles struck the people in the area. Many Cayuse children died. The Cayuse blamed the Whitmans for bringing measles to the region. A Cayuse chief ordered that the Whitmans and some other settlers be killed. A group of Cayuse killed 14 people and burned the mission buildings.

Timeline of Settlement

Early Exploration

1592 Greek explorer Juan de Fuca claims to have sailed along Washington's shore.

1792 American captain Robert Gray sails into the mouth of the Columbia River and names it after his ship.

1805 Lewis and Clark travel across the Pacific Northwest and reach the Pacific Ocean at the mouth of the Columbia River.

Further Exploration and Settlement

1807 British trader David Thompson explores the Columbia River. Four years later he becomes the first European to navigate the length of the river to the Pacific.

1824 Fort Vancouver is established by a British fur trader named John McLoughlin.

1845 An African American man named George Washington Bush, from Missouri, establishes one of the first farms near Puget Sound.

Border Agreement and Conflict

1846 The United States and Britain agree on the line that creates the northern border of Washington. Britain gives up its claim to what is now Washington.

1847 A measles epidemic kills many Cayuse children, leading to a conflict with settlers known as the Cayuse War.

1848 The U.S. Congress establishes the Oregon Territory, which at first includes what is now Washington.

Territory and Statehood

1853 The U.S. Congress establishes the Washington Territory.

1883 The Northern Pacific Railway is completed, allowing more people to travel safely to the Pacific Northwest.

1889 President Benjamin Harrison signs legislation making Washington the 42nd state on November 11.

Early Settlers

The first settlers in what is now Washington had come west for the fur trade. Fort Vancouver and Spokane House were among the first fur-trading posts in the area. In the early 1800s both the United States and Great Britain claimed the land that is now Washington. An 1846 agreement between the two countries established that it was part of the United States.

Map of Settlements and Resources in Early Washington

1 *Fort Vancouver, a fur-trading post, is established in 1824.*

4 *A steam-powered sawmill for cutting lumber is built by Henry Yesler in 1852. It is the first of its kind on Puget Sound and provides jobs for many people in the area.*

5 *A group of settlers arrives at the site of present-day Seattle in 1851. This group, known as the Denny Party, had traveled from the Midwest.*

2 *Fort Okanogan is established as a fur trading post at the junction of the Okanogan and Columbia rivers in 1811. A museum dedicated to the fur-trading industry can be seen at this spot today.*

3 *In 1845, George Washington Bush establishes one of the first farms near Puget Sound. He is thought to be the first African American settler in what is now Washington.*

6 *Missionary Marcus Whitman and his wife, Narcissa, set up a mission near present-day Walla Walla in 1836.*

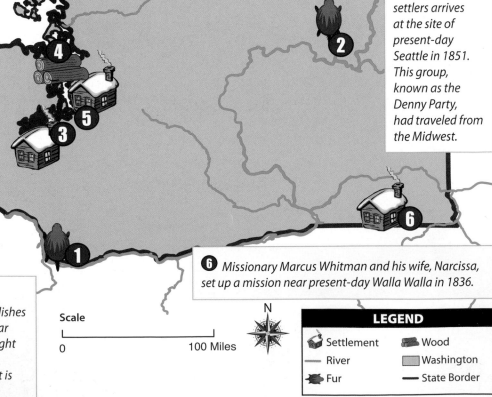

Scale

0   100 Miles

N

LEGEND

🏠 Settlement	🪵 Wood
— River	▨ Washington
🐾 Fur	— State Border

The U.S. government offered free land to any settler willing to live and work on it. In the mid-1800s people began to move to the area in large numbers. The trees in Washington were some of the biggest they had ever seen. Lumberjacks were quick to set up sawmills. It was not long before towns and cities began to grow around these sawmills.

In 1883 the Northern Pacific Railway was completed. It stretched all the way from St. Paul, Minnesota, to the Pacific Northwest. The natural resources were so plentiful that people continued to pour into the Washington region. In order to move raw materials to other regions, shipbuilding and shipping industries grew quickly.

Today, visitors can explore Fort Vancouver National Historic Site. and see a full-scale replica of the fort.

I DIDN'T KNOW THAT!

The Jesuit missionary Pierre Jean de Smet established Roman Catholic missions in what is now northeastern Washington.

The first salmon cannery in the world was established on the Columbia River at Eagle Cliff.

Early farmers in the area used teams of horses to work their fields.

A fire destroyed much of downtown Seattle in 1889.

The Whitman Mission is now a national historic site. The site includes a museum and book store.

The Northern Pacific Railway logo was created in 1893.

Notable People

Many notable people from Washington contributed to the development of their state and country. They include Indian leaders, authors, Nobel Prize winners, and the first Chinese American governor in the United States. Well-known people born in Washington even include one of the wealthiest people in the world.

CHIEF SEATTLE
(c. 1780–1866)

Chief Seattle was the leader of the Duwamish and Suquamish American Indian tribes in the Puget Sound area. When settlers arrived in the area, he established friendly relations with them. He also signed a treaty establishing two reservations for American Indians. Chief Seattle remained at peace with settlers even when other tribes went to war with them. The city of Seattle is named for him.

MARY THERESE MCCARTHY
(1912–1989)

Born in Seattle, McCarthy was orphaned at the age of six when her parents died in a flu epidemic. She moved to New York as an adult, where she became a writer and critic. Her first novel, *The Company She Keeps*, was written in 1942. She went on to write many popular books. Her novel *The Group* was a best-seller for two years after it was published in 1963. McCarthy was also well-known as a political activist.

FRANCIS SCOBEE (1939– 1986)

Francis "Dick" Scobee was born in Cle Elum. He joined the United States Air Force, and he was selected for NASA's astronaut program in 1978. He was killed commanding the space shuttle *Challenger* in 1986, along with the rest of his crew, when the craft exploded shortly after takeoff. After this disaster, his elementary school in Auburn was re-named Dick Scobee Elementary.

LINDA BUCK (1947–)

Linda Buck was born in Seattle and attended the University of Washington. She became a biologist and has done extensive research on the olfactory system, which is the system of the body involved in the sense of smell. In 2004 she was awarded the Nobel Prize in Physiology or Medicine for her work.

BILL GATES (1955–)

Seattle-born Gates met his future business partner Paul Allen in the eighth grade. At age 17, they started their own software company. The company would eventually become Microsoft. Gates became the youngest American self-made billionaire in 1987, when he was 31 years old.

I DIDN'T KNOW THAT!

George Washington Bush (c. 1778–1863) was born in Pennsylvania. He fought in the War of 1812 and settled in Missouri. In an effort to escape the **discrimination** he faced there as an African American, Bush and his wife joined several other families and headed west. In 1845, Bush became the first African American settler in what is now Washington. He and his family started a farm near Puget Sound, using seeds they had carried with them. It became the most productive farm in the area.

Gary Locke (1950–) was born in Seattle. He was elected to the state House of Representatives in 1982. In 1996, he was elected governor of Washington. He became the first Chinese American governor in the United States. In 2009, President Barack Obama appointed him U.S. secretary of commerce.

Population

At the time of the 2010 U.S. Census, Washington was home to more than 6.7 million people. Its population grew by more than 14 percent between 2000 and 2010, almost one and a half times the national average. Most Washingtonians are of European descent. Hispanic Americans make up a large cultural group in the state, accounting for more than 10 percent of the population. About 7 percent of Washingtonians are Asian American.

More than 75 percent of all the people in Washington live west of the Cascades, especially near Puget Sound. Washington's largest city, Seattle, is in this area. So is the state capital, Olympia, which was named for the Olympic Mountains.

Washington Population 1950–2010

Washington's population is almost three times as large as it was in 1950. What are some reasons that so many people have moved to Washington since then?

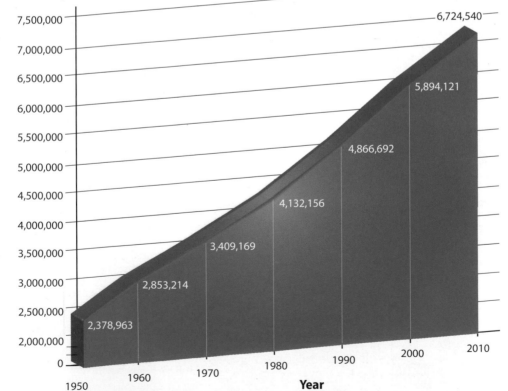

Number of People

Year	Number of People
1950	2,378,963
1960	2,853,214
1970	3,409,169
1980	4,132,156
1990	4,866,692
2000	5,894,121
2010	6,724,540

Chinese heritage is celebrated at Chinese New Year festivities throughout the state.

American Indians make up about 2 percent of Washington's population.

The Yakama Nation Museum and Cultural Center holds a three-day celebration every June. The celebration is kicked off with a parade. The festivities include dancing, games, and contests.

In 1962, a Chinese American man named Wing Luke became the first Asian American to hold an elected office in Washington when he won a Seattle City Council seat.

More than 615,000 people live in Seattle. The second-largest city is Spokane, and the third largest city is Tacoma. Both have populations of around 200,000 people. In recent years, some Washingtonians have moved away from the big cities, choosing instead to live in the countryside or on the San Juan Islands in the northwestern corner of the state.

More than 616,000 people live in Washington's largest city, Seattle.

Politics and Government

The government of Washington is centered in Olympia, the capital. There are three branches of the state government. The first is the executive. This branch decides how the state's money will be spent. It also ensures that laws made by the state are carried out. The governor, who is elected to a four-year term, is head of this branch. The lieutenant governor, the secretary of state, the attorney general, and the treasurer serve under the governor in the executive branch.

The second branch is the legislative branch, or state legislature. This branch makes the laws of the state. Washington's legislature is called the General Assembly, and it consists of two chambers, or parts. They are the Senate, which has 49 members, and the House of Representatives, which has 98.

The Jefferson County Court House was completed in 1892. According to state legend, the bell in its clock tower was drawn into position by a white horse.

The judicial branch consists of all the courts of the state. These include local courts as well as the state's highest court, the Supreme Court. The judicial branch ensures that citizens of the state obey the laws.

Like all states, Washington is represented in the U.S. Congress in Washington, D.C. Each state elects two U.S. senators, who serve six-year terms. The number of people a state sends to the U.S. House of Representatives is determined by population. Starting in 2013, Washington will have 10 representatives in the House. This is one more than it had in the previous 10 years. U.S. representatives serve two-year terms.

The Washington state capitol building in Olympia is open to the public for tours.

Washington's state song is called "Washington, My Home."

Here is an excerpt from the song:

This is my country; God gave it to me;
I will protect it, Ever keep it free.
Small towns and cities rest here in the sun,
Filled with our laughter. Thy will be done.

Washington my home;
Where ever I may roam;
This is my land, my native land, Washington, my home.
As people always free.
For you and me a destiny;
Washington my home.
For you and me a destiny;
Washington my home.

Cultural Groups

Although their numbers are small, American Indians add much to the culture of Washington. Some Americans Indians in the area lost touch with their early traditions when settlers of European descent arrived. Most were forced to move to reservations. Today the state's American Indians are trying to bring their traditional culture back to life. For instance, American Indians along the Washington coast are known for their beautiful and colorful totem poles, which they carve in the traditional style. Also, the Northwest Museum of Arts & Culture in Spokane displays items and artifacts that represent the cultures that once flourished in the area.

Many of Washington's early settlers came from England, Germany, and the Scandinavian countries of Norway, Sweden, and Denmark. Seattle has many residents of Scandinavian descent, especially in a district known as Ballard. Among the many Scandinavian features of Ballard is a large mural that was donated by the king and queen of Norway in 1996.

The Yakama reservation covers more than one million acres in south-central Washington.

In the 1960s the town of Leavenworth was rebuilt to look like a traditional German village.

Washington has had a large Asian population since its early days. In the 1800s Japanese and Chinese workers helped build railroads. They also planted orchards, worked in factories, and fished in the area. More Asian people have moved to the state in recent decades. Many have come from Vietnam, the Philippines, South Korea, and Thailand.

The Seattle Asian Art Museum has one of the most extensive collections of Asian art in the country.

I DIDN'T KNOW THAT!

Each fall the German community of Leavenworth holds its own variation of the popular Oktoberfest held in Munich, Germany.

Japanese art and culture is celebrated at the Cherry Blossom and Japanese Cultural Festival in Seattle, held every April.

Seafair is the largest community festival in the Pacific Northwest. It is held in Seattle every summer.

People of Scandinavian descent in Poulsbo celebrate Viking Fest each May. It includes a parade and Norwegian food and entertainment.

Many African Americans and Hispanics came to Washington during World War II to find work.

Arts and Entertainment

Much like other states of the Pacific Northwest, Washington offers plenty to do in the great outdoors. Hiking, skiing, snowboarding, kayaking, rock climbing, bicycling, and camping are especially popular.

For those who prefer the arts, the state offers both indoor and outdoor arts venues. Seattle is the biggest cultural center in Washington. It has some of the state's top museums, including the Seattle Art Museum and the Pacific Science Center. Seattle also hosts a yearly arts festival called Bumbershoot. The Bumbershoot festival takes place during the Labor Day weekend and features dance, music, theater, and comedy shows.

Jimi Hendrix, the famous guitar player and rock singer of the 1960s, was from Seattle.

Hardly a month goes by in Washington when there is not a festival of some kind. Music, sports, and international festivals highlight different aspects of the state. The Central Washington State Fair takes place in Yakima every year. Cheney hosts a festival called Rodeo Days in July. In Port Townsend, the Washington State Arts Commission founded an arts center called Centrum in 1973. Centrum hosts music festivals, concerts, and workshops.

Arts and crafts fairs can be found across the state throughout the year. American Indians still practice many of their traditional arts and crafts. Crafts such as beadwork, carving, and basket making are very popular. The Pacific Northwest Arts Fair held in Bellevue is one of the largest in the state.

Actress Anna Faris grew up in Edmonds. She made her professional acting debut at the Seattle Repertory Theater at age nine.

Actor Rainn Wilson, who became well-known to millions of viewers as the character Dwight in the TV sit-com *The Office*, attended Shorecrest High School in Shoreline. He played clarinet and bassoon in the school band.

Gary Larson, the cartoonist who created "The Far Side," grew up in Tacoma.

Bing Crosby, the singer and actor who popularized the song "White Christmas," was born in Tacoma and grew up in Spokane. There is now a Crosby Student Center at Gonzaga University, which is in Spokane.

Author Raymond Carver grew up in Yakima. *Everything Must Go*, a movie based on one of Carver's short stories, stars Will Ferrell.

In 1974 Spokane hosted a World's Fair. It was the smallest city ever to do so.

Sports

Sports are an important form of entertainment in Washington. If people are not taking part in a sport themselves, they will likely be watching the state's professional teams. Washington's professional teams are all based in Seattle.

The Seattle Seahawks are members of the National Football League. The Seahawks played temporarily at the University of Washington until their new stadium, Qwest Field, opened in 2004. The new stadium was also designed to host soccer games. The state's baseball team is the Seattle Mariners. Mariners outfielder Ichiro Suzuki holds two major league records. He has the most hits in a season and the most seasons in a row with at least 200 hits. Seattle is also home to the Seattle Storm women's basketball team. The team is part of the Women's National Basketball Association, or WNBA. In 2010, the Storm won the WNBA championship. The team's center, Lauren Jackson, was named the league's Most Valuable Player for both the regular season and the finals.

Seattle Mariners outfielder Ichiro Suzuki donated more than $1 million to Japanese relief efforts after a devastating earthquake and tsunami hit Japan in 2011.

College-level sports are also popular across the state. Football is big on the University of Washington campus. The Huskies won the Rose Bowl seven times between 1960 and 2003. More than 70,000 fans attend the team's home games. Both the men's and the women's rowing teams at the University of Washington have won numerous national titles.

Seattle Storm team member Lauren Jackson is one of the best-known players in the WNBA. She has been named the league's Most Valuable Player three times.

National Averages Comparison

The United States is a federal republic, consisting of fifty states and the District of Columbia. Alaska and Hawai'i are the only non-contiguous, or non-touching, states in the nation. Today, the United States of America is the third-largest country in the world in population. The United States Census Bureau takes a census, or count of all the people, every ten years. It also regularly collects other kinds of data about the population and the economy. How does Washington compare to the national average?

Comparison Chart

United States 2010 Census Data *	USA	Washington
Admission to Union	NA	November 11, 1889
Land Area (in square miles)	3,537,438.44	66,544.06
Population Total	308,745,538	6,724,540
Population Density (people per square mile)	87.28	101.05
Population Percentage Change (April 1, 2000, to April 1, 2010)	9.7%	14.1%
White Persons (percent)	72.4%	77.3%
Black Persons (percent)	12.6%	3.6%
American Indian and Alaska Native Persons (percent)	0.9%	1.5%
Asian Persons (percent)	4.8%	7.2%
Native Hawaiian and Other Pacific Islander Persons (percent)	0.2%	0.6%
Some Other Race (percent)	6.2%	5.2%
Persons Reporting Two or More Races (percent)	2.9%	4.7%
Persons of Hispanic or Latino Origin (percent)	16.3%	11.2%
Not of Hispanic or Latino Origin (percent)	83.7%	88.8%
Median Household Income	$52,029	$58,081
Percentage of People Age 25 or Over Who Have Graduated from High School	80.4%	87.1%

*All figures are based on the 2010 United States Census, with the exception of the last two items. Percentages may not add to 100 because of rounding.

How to Improve My Community

Strong communities make strong states. Think about what features are important in your community. What do you value? Education? Health? Forests? Safety? Beautiful spaces? Government works to help citizens create ideal living conditions that are fair to all by providing services in communities. Consider what changes you could make in your community. How would they improve your state as a whole? Using this concept web as a guide, write a report that outlines the features you think are most important in your community and what improvements could be made. A strong state needs strong communities.

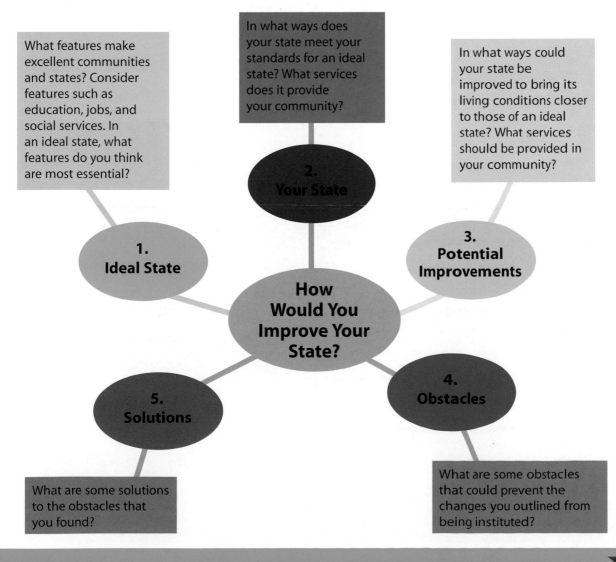

What features make excellent communities and states? Consider features such as education, jobs, and social services. In an ideal state, what features do you think are most essential?

In what ways does your state meet your standards for an ideal state? What services does it provide your community?

In what ways could your state be improved to bring its living conditions closer to those of an ideal state? What services should be provided in your community?

2.
Your State

1.
Ideal State

3.
Potential Improvements

How Would You Improve Your State?

5.
Solutions

4.
Obstacles

What are some solutions to the obstacles that you found?

What are some obstacles that could prevent the changes you outlined from being instituted?

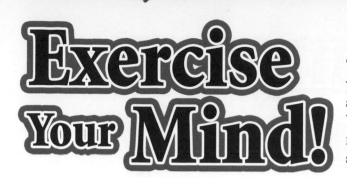

Exercise Your Mind!

Think about these questions and then use your research skills to find the answers and learn more fascinating facts about Washington. A teacher, librarian, or parent may be able to help you locate the best sources to use in your research.

1 Washington is covered with parkland. How much land do state-run parks occupy?

2 Which American Indian is known for helping the famed explorers Lewis and Clark?

3 How long did it take to build the Grand Coulee Dam?

4 What is a young salmon called?

5 Which famous football quarterback is from Washington?

6 What is Bill Gates's full name?

7 What warning signs were there that Mount St. Helens was about to erupt in 1980?

8 What Seattle rock band is given credit for creating grunge music?

Words to Know

aerospace industry: the research, design, and production of airplanes, missiles, and spacecraft

archipelago: a chain of islands

commercial: for profit, or to make money

contiguous: all connected to or touching one another

deplete: to decrease a supply or resource

discrimination: unfair treatment, often based on race

endangered: in danger of dying out

environmentalists: people who work to protect the Earth, including the environment, plants, and animals

grunge: alternative rock music from the early 1990s

hydroelectric power: electricity produced by using the power of flowing water

olivine: any member of a group of common magnesium minerals, usually green in color

plentiful: abundant

reservation: an area of land set aside for American Indians

vegetation: plant life

Index

Log on to www.av2books.com

AV² by Weigl brings you media enhanced books that support active learning. Go to www.av2books.com, and enter the special code found on page 2 of this book. You will gain access to enriched and enhanced content that supplements and complements this book. Content includes video, audio, web links, quizzes, a slide show, and activities.

Audio
Listen to sections of the book read aloud.

Video
Watch informative video clips.

Embedded Weblinks
Gain additional information for research.

Try This!
Complete activities and hands-on experiments.

WHAT'S ONLINE?

Try This!	Embedded Weblinks	Video	EXTRA FEATURES
Test your knowledge of the state in a mapping activity.	Discover more attractions in Washington.	Watch a video introduction to Washington.	**Audio** Listen to sections of the book read aloud.
Find out more about precipitation in your city.	Learn more about the history of the state.	Watch a video about the features of the state.	**Key Words** Study vocabulary, and complete a matching word activity.
Plan what attractions you would like to visit in the state.	Learn the full lyrics of the state song.		**Slide Show** View images and captions, and prepare a presentation.
Learn more about the early natural resources of the state.			**Quizzes** Test your knowledge.
Write a biography about a notable resident of Washington.			
Complete an educational census activity.			

AV² was built to bridge the gap between print and digital. We encourage you to tell us what you like and what you want to see in the future.
Sign up to be an AV² Ambassador at www.av2books.com/ambassador.

Due to the dynamic nature of the Internet, some of the URLs and activities provided as part of AV² by Weigl may have changed or ceased to exist. AV² by Weigl accepts no responsibility for any such changes. All media enhanced books are regularly monitored to update addresses and sites in a timely manner. Contact AV² by Weigl at 1-866-649-3445 or av2books@weigl.com with any questions, comments, or feedback.